D0810470

I know this to be true

NELSON MANDELA
FOUNDATION

Living the legacy

Nelson Mandela

I know this to be true

guiding
principles

Sello Hatang
& Verne Harris

CHRONICLE BOOKS
SAN FRANCISCO

in association with

Blackwell&Ruth.

Dedicated to the legacy
and memory of
Nelson Mandela

Contents

'Good leaders fully appreciate that the removal of tensions in society . . . puts creative thinkers on centre stage by creating an ideal environment for men and women of vision to influence society.'

– Nelson Mandela

Introduction

This little book is the result of years of discussion between the two of us, and dialogue with others, about the question of what lessons the leadership of Nelson Mandela offers. Not everyone can endure more than twenty-seven years in prison. Not everyone can lead a liberation movement. Not everyone can be president. But what can *anyone* take from Mandela's example in order to find the leader inside themselves? This question has challenged us through a decade of leadership development endeavour. One of us, Verne, worked in African National Congress structures while Mandela led a complex negotiation process with the apartheid state. Both of us worked in government when Madiba was president of South Africa.[i] One of us, Sello, held a senior position in the South African Human Rights Commission at a time when Madiba was using his influence as a leader to challenge structures of power on a range of issues close to his heart. Both of us became employees of his post-presidential office. Both of us worked on the formation of his private archive, read deeply in it, and engaged him personally in the process. This little book represents what we've learned.

Sello Hatang and Verne Harris

'The world is full of people with natural leadership qualities.'

– Nelson Mandela

Prologue

It is 1986. South Africa is in a State of Emergency which will hold the country in a vice-like grip for another four years. Nelson Mandela is in Pollsmoor Prison near Cape Town,[ii] newly separated from other long-term political prisoners and beginning to engage senior representatives of the apartheid regime in preliminary 'talks about talks'.[iii] It is a moment fraught with danger for Mandela. He has made the first moves without consulting his colleagues and then continues against their counsel and with very little access to the leadership of his organization (the African National Congress) outside the country. The regime deploys intelligence operatives, psychiatrists and other analysts to extract maximum advantage from the moment. They document everything Mandela is doing and record all his conversations.

For Mandela the leader, this is a point of no return. If he allows the regime to drive a wedge between him and the external leadership, or if he makes unsanctioned concessions, or if the process he is leading unravels parallel processes being overseen by the African National Congress (ANC), then he will be fatally compromised. Colleagues in the movement who know about the process worry for him. They fear the worst. Arguably the whole trajectory of his life hinges on this moment.

Mandela does not falter.

'He didn't make a false step,' recalled George Bizos many years later. Bizos was one of Mandela's lawyers, visiting him frequently at the time and providing a vital conduit between him and the ANC leadership in exile. 'He was completely in charge.'[1]

'The mark of great leaders is the ability to understand the context in which they are operating and act accordingly.'

– Nelson Mandela

A Great Leader

What made Nelson Mandela the leader he became? Why did he become a global icon of great leadership? Was it because he never put a foot wrong? Did he have almost saintly qualities rarely found in a single human being? We don't think so. Neither did he. By his own admission, he made mistakes, both political and personal. He had weaknesses, even flaws. He was, at best, in the memorable words he used as he started drafting a new memoir in 1998, 'a sinner who keeps on trying'.

Attempts to identify the defining qualities of Mandela as a leader are legion. Most fall into the trap of positioning him in relation to what could be called generic attributes of leadership – vision, courage, the ability to keep one's rivals close, knowing when to step away and so on. In 2007, the Nelson Mandela Foundation, to its cost, did exactly this. Mandela was in the process of withdrawing from public life. He had given the Foundation a new mandate for social justice work, and in preparing to implement it, the Foundation, amongst other things, sought to identify what were called the core values informing his life and work. A team of independent researchers and analysts worked with Foundation staff on the project, convening focus groups and conducting deep interviews with twenty-three individuals who had worked closely with Mandela at different periods in his life. Mandela's personal archive was studied – diaries, notebooks, private correspondence and more. What emerged was a compelling absence of consensus. The complexity of Nelson Mandela the human being simply refused to be reduced to a series of neatly labelled boxes – the seven steps to effective leadership, or whatever.

For the truth is that we have to dig deeper if we want to find the key to understanding Mandela's leadership. In those depths, a willingness to embrace complexity, even contradiction, is essential. So, for example, most representations of his life foreground his commitment to collective leadership and his willingness to consult. And yet stories abound of moments, big and small, when he acted against advice or without it. That moment in Pollsmoor Prison is but one of them. Arguably, great leaders are defined precisely by their ability to identify when this approach is necessary. Another example: For many interpreters of Mandela, he embodied the principle of delegation, and during his presidency he perfected this art as he left the day-to-day running of government to his lieutenants while he focused on the big-picture dimensions of policy, strategy and symbolic intervention. And yet the evidence shows that in many areas of governance he was hands-on, almost a prototypical chief executive, even guilty of micromanaging at times.

We could go on endlessly with examples of complexity. Mandela was a politician's politician, nimble, even at times opportunistic. And yet he was deeply principled. And he could also be inflexible, even stubborn. Mandela was a peacemaker, a reconciler. But he was also a freedom fighter and an expert exponent of brinkmanship. Mandela believed in the liberatory power of education and promoted access to it at every turn and in every way possible. At the same time, former associates of his have identified his tendency to fetishize formal qualifications and have critiqued his school-building programme as a misguided philanthropic intervention which failed to address the deep, systemic problems with South Africa's education system. It is undeniable that under Mandela's watch the first post-apartheid administration attempted to transform this system using models and strategies primarily from the global North. These proved ineffective, and arguably inappropriate, in the context of 1990s South Africa. In our view – and we both worked in government during Mandela's presidency – across the public sector at that time there was a confidence that anything could be fixed, and quickly, using only global best-practice benchmarks. This hubris was linked to a notion of South African exceptionalism and a certain resistance to learning deeply from the experiences of the global South.

Simplifying Mandela, romanticizing him, is not helpful. Goodness knows there is enough of that in both local and international discourses. Arguably it is this which underlies, even provokes, a counter-current discernible especially amongst younger people. This current is impatient with seamless triumphalist marches and suggests that Mandela and his generation of leaders sold out black South

Africans during the negotiation of democracy. Many voices articulating this current pit him against his former wife Winnie Madikizela-Mandela, with him as villain and her as heroine. What is both helpful and necessary is respect for evidence and a willingness to engage with complex pasts and personalities. When Mandela donated his personal archive to the Nelson Mandela Foundation he made it clear that it was not to become the basis for a vanity project, nor were the custodians to carry the burden of protecting him. The archive was to be a public resource, the overarching purpose of which was to contribute to making the country, and the world, of his dreams.

What, then, made Nelson Mandela the leader he became? What does the evidence tell us? If there is no clutch of 'Mandela core leadership attributes', then where do we find the lessons for good leadership from his life? What do we find when we dig deeper? As a leader, Nelson Mandela had an extraordinary sense of timing. He seemed to have an instinct for knowing when he should lead from behind, the shepherd behind his flock, and when he should be out front. He was fond of quoting the Thembu regent who mentored him as a youth after his father's death:[iv] 'I always remember the regent's axiom: a leader, he said, is like a shepherd. He stays behind the flock letting the most nimble go on ahead, whereupon the others follow, not realising that all along they are being directed from behind.'[2] And yet Mandela seemed more comfortable when leading from the front. He had a fine instinct for knowing when to give ground and when to take it. When to wait, and when to move. Arguably his genius was that most often he got it right. Trying to explain instinct is futile, of course. It is what it is. But what is the space within which good timing and instinct are most likely to flourish?

In the case of Nelson Mandela, we would argue, this fecund space was one he fashioned out of what we would call discipline and principle. His daily disciplines of conduct, routine and practice hold the key to understanding why he became such an effective and admirable leader. These are disciplines anyone can learn. And everyone can use them to help in finding the leader within themselves.

'It is absolutely necessary at times for the leader to take an independent action without consulting anybody and to present what he has done to the organisation.'

– Nelson Mandela

'We have been brought up in the tradition of collective leadership. We discuss matters thoroughly, differ sometimes very sharply but eventually we reach a consensus.'

– Nelson Mandela

Discipline and Principle

By the time he became president of South
Africa, Mandela had developed an enormous
capacity to listen to others. Unlike so many
prominent people, his instinct seemed to
be to listen to someone else rather than
give them a lecture. Whether famous or
unknown, accomplished or humble, those
who encountered him felt they had his ear.
At one level, one could argue, he simply had
a genuine interest in the lives and thoughts
of those he encountered. But there was a
deeper, very deliberate, discipline at play. He
had been born into traditions of collectivity
which prized the art of listening and demanded
of everyone a respect for rituals of consultation
and dialogue. He had been schooled in these
rituals through childhood and youth by his
parents and abaThembu elders.[v] Even leaders
at the highest level spent more time listening
than talking. Induction into the ANC and the
broader Congress movement added another
layer of learning – he rose quickly through the
ranks, at each step becoming honed in the
practice of working in collective structures.[vi]

While in prison he taught himself to listen intently to the voices of the enemy. He read widely on the history of Afrikaner nationalism. He became proficient in Afrikaans. This gave him a resource which he used skilfully in fighting for ever-greater rights for prisoners. For instance, he was able to draw on his knowledge of prison conditions for Afrikaner nationalists incarcerated after the rebellion of 1914 to leverage concessions from the apartheid state. And in the 1980s in Pollsmoor when he inaugurated 'talks about talks' he was able to draw on a fundamental power he had crafted over years of painstaking practice. But he engaged at levels beyond pragmatism, or even courtesy, with the prison warders.[vii] He chose to be interested in their lives. He listened. He took the lead in connecting. And in doing so he embodied a generosity which is arguably the very possibility of ethics.

Finding the generosity of listening became more challenging for him in later years as his powers were waning, but his diary[viii] remained cluttered by myriads of people seeking an audience with him. And relatively few of them were there to listen to him; rather, they were there to press him for favours. We remember one occasion, exemplary of the challenges faced by him, when Jack Warner was in town and wanting to see him. Warner was a candidate in an election campaign back in Trinidad and Tobago and had announced to local media that he was seeking Mandela's endorsement. On arrival at the Nelson Mandela Foundation, Warner and his two assistants were asked to sign undertakings not to discuss the campaign with Mandela. Warner refused and stalked out of the building without seeing him. Nonetheless, Mandela agreed to spend time with the assistants, who had signed, and proceeded to listen to their long, mundane tales of travel and travail.

Nelson Mandela could give a long speech when he felt it was needed. He is renowned for a number of epoch-making ones – the 'black man in a white man's court' speeches of 1962, his 1964 'I am prepared to die' speech at the Rivonia Trial,[ix] the 1990 speech on his release from prison, his address to the nation in 1993 after the assassination of Chris Hani,[x] his inauguration speech in 1994 and so on.[3]

He could speak with great eloquence and power when the occasion demanded it, but as a rule, and as a discipline, he seldom wasted words. 'It is never my custom to use words lightly,' he once said. 'If twenty-seven years in prison have done anything to us, it was to use the silence of solitude to make us understand how precious words are and how real speech is in its impact on the way people live and die.'[4] We heard him more than once in later life asking (usually after having had to listen to an overlong speech), 'Why take ten minutes to say what could be said in one?'

Humanity

Despite his long walk to freedom being full of pain and deprivation, Nelson Mandela believed in the fundamental goodness of human beings and, in the words of long-time associate and friend Jakes Gerwel, 'he conducts himself consistently in accordance with that view'. This was another discipline, if you like, a practice of *ubuntu* fused with other influences. Gerwel, writing in 2008, elaborates:

*Madiba has almost something of a
nineteenth-century positivist faith in
empirical science; and he bases his
acceptance of the basic goodness of
people on it. He once observed that
if people's daily lives . . . could be
monitored, it would be determined
empirically that most people are good
as a rule, doing extremely bad things
only as an exception. Why model your
human relations on an expectation of
the exceptional he asks.*[5]

For Mandela, the great scourges of humanity –
prejudice, hatred and greed – were learned
behaviours and could be unlearned:

*No one is born hating another person
because of the colour of his skin, or his
background, or his religion. People must
learn to hate, and if they can learn to
hate, they can be taught to love, for love
comes more naturally to the human heart
than its opposite.*[6]

Education was the key for him. People can learn to be good, as they can learn not to be ignorant.

It was easy, then, for Mandela to believe the best of another, of every other, until he was proved wrong. This discipline of generosity, fused with a long practice of comradeship in his political movement, formed the basis of his loyalty in personal relationships. Inevitably there is a shadow to this discipline. Mandela could be too loyal. He could choose not to see the shortcomings of comrades and associates. He could tolerate too long the evidence of wrongdoing. He could give a second chance one too many times.

Belief in a fundamental human goodness did not blind Mandela to complexity. In 1979, in a letter to his wife Winnie, he mused: 'In real life we deal, not with gods, but with ordinary humans like ourselves: men and women who are full of contradictions, who are stable and fickle, strong and weak, famous and infamous, people in whose bloodstream the muckworm battles daily with potent pesticides.'[7] Not for him the need to identify one as good and another as bad. Instead, he had an almost post-positivist perspective on the human experience of wrestling with the 'strangers inside'.

Pain

Mandela's long walk to freedom was by definition a passage with and through pain. However, he chose to see pain not as bad, but as simply painful. He chose to ask what he owed life rather than what life owed him. He chose to learn from pain. And, to echo Gerwel's words in this context, he conducted himself consistently in accordance with that choice. This was a principle which translated into a discipline of conduct. One which stood him in good stead as he took the blows of unspeakable loss through an extremely long life – he lost his father at a very young age, he lost his own children, some early, some late in life, grandchildren, beloved comrades. He lost two marriages. Who can forget that wrenching moment in 1992 when he called a press conference and announced his separation from Winnie Madikizela-Mandela? Here was no

'We need the commitment of leaders at all levels in order to achieve the better life for all that we promised our people.'

– Nelson Mandela

hiding from pain. Here was almost an embrace of it, with the determination to make a new life, to keep going, to keep working. And who can forget that seminal moment when at the death of his son Makgatho he announced to the world that this loss was a manifestation of South Africa's HIV/AIDS scourge?[xi] His pain had become a weapon against taboo.

His long years in prison were not wasted. He turned the pain of separation from loved ones into a sustained nurturing of intimacy with them from afar. In ways that he had not been able to do when he was caught up in the exigencies and demands of struggle, he cared for domestic space, engaging with even the mundane details of family members through every means available to him, including a rich and increasingly abundant correspondence. In an act of will, as we've already argued, he made incarceration a space within which he learned the language of the oppressor, a learning critical to his later role as leader of negotiations. And his actions in Pollsmoor in 1986 were a demonstration of how years of pain can be honed into a liberatory instrument.[xii]

During his ninetieth year, in a quiet moment of reflection with his personal assistant Zelda la Grange, Mandela said, 'Robben Island, I like it very much[xiii] . . . it was a totally different experience . . . I was happy that I went through it.'[8] At one level, he was expressing nostalgia for a period in his life when he had had lots of time for reading, writing and reflection. A period in which he enjoyed slow daily rhythms, an absence of clutter and a powerful camaraderie with friends he loved. A period in which he was not yet a prisoner of his own fame. At another level, he was simply demonstrating what can be learned from pain.

Taking Responsibility

Arguably the real test of leadership takes place when individuals and collectivities have to respond to things going awry, mistakes being made or plans not working out. Avoiding failed endeavour is not fundamental to good leadership; taking responsibility for it is. Doing so as a principle of conduct characterized the life and work of Nelson Mandela. He understood that falling is unavoidable on any long and rocky path. One's determination to get back up and keep on going is what counts.

Because of what he achieved in life,
it is easy to assume that everything came
easily to him.

Enormously gifted as he was, however,
there were areas of life in which failure was
not uncommon for him. Two broken marriages
forced him to dig deep. The challenges of
part-time study and of study in conditions of
incarceration were daunting. It is well known that
Mandela completed a Bachelor's degree through
the universities of Fort Hare and South Africa,
secured a postgraduate diploma in law, finished
his articles and ultimately set up a successful law
firm in partnership with O. R. Tambo.[xiv] What isn't
widely known is that Mandela wanted to have
a law degree, an LLB, and off and on for over
four decades worked at attaining it. In 1943 he
failed all his first-year courses at the University
of the Witwatersrand. By the time he was finally
awarded the degree by the University of South
Africa in 1989, he had failed more than thirty law
courses. His capacity to keep going, to work
with failure, simply to endure, was extraordinary.
As was his refusal years later when reflecting
on this long saga to blame circumstances:
'I was not a bright student,' he insisted.[9]

He knew how to bear the weight of the buck stopping with him. At the end of his presidency he acknowledged that he had not done enough to fight the scourge of HIV/AIDS. A large part of his energy and time in the post-presidential period were dedicated to the fight – it was to take him into a difficult, and very public, clash with his successor, Thabo Mbeki,[xv] over policy and strategy. Bearing the weight was a habit. During the first democratic election campaign, for instance, violent clashes between Inkatha Freedom Party (IFP) supporters and ANC security at Shell House saw many killed.[xvi] Mandela insisted on taking responsibility for the order to fire in defence of the building. Also during that campaign, he surprised everybody by calling publicly for the voting age to be reduced to fourteen. There was consternation in the collective ANC leadership, and in a meeting shortly thereafter Mandela was taken to task by his colleagues. He painstakingly made notes as each one critiqued him. His final note acknowledges that he had made a bad error of judgement.

One last example of him taking responsibility in his capacity as a leader relates to the country's rugby administration. In 1995, Mandela had taken a huge political risk by supporting the retention of the Springbok emblem in the run-up to the Rugby World Cup later that year, and by associating closely with the then-president of the South African Rugby Union (SARU), Louis Luyt. Two years later the failures of transformation within rugby forced Mandela to appoint a commission of enquiry into the sport's administration. Luyt responded by bringing a court application to have the commission withdrawn. Against the counsel of his advisers, Mandela obeyed a subpoena to give evidence in court and subjected himself to rough cross-questioning from Luyt's legal team. He knew how to do the dirty work.

This was his habit, his discipline, in private life as well. Just one example will make the point. In 1958, he was acting as the defence attorney in a prominent human rights case in Johannesburg. His comrade Ruth First, brilliant and easily intimidating, was critical of the way he was handling the case.[xvii] One day she phoned him and conveyed her views. Mandela was hurt, angry, and told her to 'go to hell'. Later that day, he drove across to where she worked at the University of the Witwatersrand and apologized with a hug.

Liberating Oneself

Nelson Mandela was a freedom fighter. He knew how to serve. Arguably he sacrificed both 'the personal' and 'the domestic' to the demands of 'the movement', 'the people' and 'the struggle'. His life was, almost quintessentially, one of service. At the same time, however, it was one of self-liberation, perhaps the most difficult of all journeys. His life, in our view, exemplified the maxim 'You need an army to liberate a country, but only you can liberate yourself'. This was a maxim also articulated – in different modes and registers – by Bantu Stephen Biko and the Black Consciousness Movement.[xviii]

Mandela was shaped by multiple traditions, institutions and mentors. But what he demonstrated from very early on was a capacity to test every rule taught to him and either adopt it as his own or discard it. Not for him an unthinking acceptance of orthodoxy. As a teenager he went through circumcision

'Amongst my generation there are many that could have taken my place if circumstance and history had determined differently. Where I gave leadership it was because of those that surrounded me and formed me.'

– Nelson Mandela

and other related rites of passage. In later life he confessed to having broken the rule not 'to look back' as his cohort put their initiation huts to the torch and headed back into the world as men.[10] And later in life he continued to break rules of tradition by violating the taboo on disclosing secrets of initiation. As an old man he advised his grandsons to be circumcised not in the mountain but in hospital. Crucially, in terms of his life trajectory, as a young man he made two life-changing decisions within months of each other. First, he defied the principal of the University of Fort Hare, thus effectively expelling himself, and then he defied the Thembu regent when the latter informed him that he had been promised in marriage to a young woman in the kingdom. Mandela stole two oxen from the regent and used the proceeds to fund his journey to a new life in Johannesburg.

The work of liberating oneself never ends. He and his old comrade Ahmed Kathrada would often reminisce about their first encounter with HIV/AIDS while in Pollsmoor Prison in the 1980s.[xix] Both were vulnerable to the myths and taboos which swirled around the issue and the people who were positive. They worried, for instance, about contracting the disease through any form of physical contact. Both worked hard subsequently to inform themselves about the nature and the scope of the pandemic. Mandela's notebooks from the early 1990s have many entries on the topic, and he continued developing his understanding until the end of his life.

When it comes to patriarchy, Mandela was in many ways a product of his time and place. In 2005, he was to look back on his life and confess that by the age of fourty-four, when he went into prison, he was still a male chauvinist. It took years of reading, reflection and discussion with comrades to understand this fully and to think about effective strategies for combatting sexism in all its forms:

> *Well, you know, sitting down in jail and reading you discover things which you have never known, outside, and that is the one advantage of being in prison, to read literature that opens your mind and makes you realize that some of your ideas in the past were completely wrong.*[11]

After his release from prison, Mandela was
to be reminded often by the strong women
close to him that he still had work to do in
translating ideas into practice. This was one
of the reasons he resisted initially his elevation
to the presidency, urging his organisation
to look to a younger man or woman for the
position. The principle, for him, was clear.
Men and women are equal. And the discipline
meant commitment to making it a reality,
day in and day out.

Humour

In later life Mandela was renowned for his
warmth and his humour. He knew how to
make people laugh. With those close to
him, he loved nothing better than the give-
and-take of teasing and the re-telling of old
jokes. He was, in short, full of mischief. We
remember him entering the Nelson Mandela
Foundation auditorium once for a public event
and spotting his old comrade Mac Maharaj
sitting in the front row.[xx] After years of being
a smoker Mac had finally kicked the habit.
With a gleam in his eye, Mandela asked Mac,

'Have you started smoking again?' Mac said no. 'But I know you,' Mandela responded, 'you're smoking dagga now.'[xxi]

But for Mandela joking could be a serious thing. A discipline. When asked in 2005 by Tim Couzens about the origins of his sense of humour, Mandela indicated that he had grown up in chiefly and royal milieus which encouraged 'seriousness'.[xxii] And that he had learned to take himself seriously, to be dignified, to have gravitas. Humour had become almost a gift he gave to those in need:

> *I like to make jokes even when examining serious situations. Because when people are relaxed they can think properly . . . we have learned from the countryside to make people happy by making jokes and making them forget about their painful experiences. It's very important.*[12]

He knew how to make people laugh. More importantly, he came to know how to laugh at himself. Stories of the young Mandela taking himself too seriously abound. In 1998, he offered this self-reflection: 'As a young man I . . . combined all the weaknesses, errors and indiscretions of a country boy . . . I relied on arrogance in order to hide my weaknesses.'[13]

For the older Mandela, the self-deprecating gesture, the disclaimer and the outright joke at one's own expense became almost tools of his trade. We remember the day he was given an advance copy of his book *Conversations with Myself* and immediately began reminiscing with Ahmed Kathrada. Turning to an extract from his 1962 diary, he recounted how he had told his Algerian military trainers that he'd never handled a gun before and consequently how impressed they were at his prowess the first time they took him to a shooting range. The two old men laughed heartily. Mandela *had* handled a gun before. He was just protecting his reputation, and his vanity, with the Algerians.

Increasingly over the years, as Mandela aged, his own frailty became the object of his humour. In 2006, when he met Sir Alex Ferguson and the Manchester United football team, for instance, he was launching into a story which was best kept out of the public domain. Alerted to this, Mandela paused, then said to the gathering, 'Sorry chaps, if I tell you this story I'll lose my job.' Some years later, one of us had to escort him down the long passage from his office to the front entrance of the Foundation, where there was to be a photo opportunity with the media. He was heavy on the arm by the time we reached the then Chief Executive Achmat Dangor at the entrance, waiting to take Mandela out. 'Ah, Achmat,' Mandela said to him, 'now you can do some *real* work!'

Also as the years advanced, he would sometimes smile at his personal assistant or another staff member when he was with visitors, and say 'You are my warder now'. It was at once a gentle tease and an indication that a still crowded diary and its many keepers meant that he was not yet free to do whatever he wanted to. He had become a prisoner of his fame and of his frailty.

'It is a grave error for any leader to be oversensitive in the face of criticism, to conduct discussions as if he or she is a schoolmaster talking to less informed and inexperienced learners.'

– Nelson Mandela

Record-keeping

Throughout most of his adult life Nelson
Mandela was an obsessive creator of
records. Partly it had to do with a certain
obsessiveness in his character. Partly it had
to do with his love for the craft of writing.
He never learned to use a computer, and by
and large avoided the typewriter. For him it
was about a discipline of penmanship. And
partly it had to do with his understanding that
record-making, like listening, gave him access
to a fundamental power. There are expansive
sociological and archival literatures which
demonstrate record-making, both in its 'paper
shuffling' and 'bit crunching' forms, to be, in
the formulation of French thinker Bruno Latour,
'the source of an essential power'.[14]

We can speculate about the origins and
influences which shaped Mandela's own
practice. His mission school and university
education, for instance. The disciplines of
legal study and of law. The privations of a long
incarceration. All, no doubt, were at play, as
well as the force of his own character. The
practice could, and did, get him into trouble.

While underground and leading an armed struggle, he kept detailed notes of his readings and his reflections. Throughout 1962, he kept a diary as he travelled through Africa, received training as a soldier, and visited ANC comrades in London. Many of these records surfaced as evidence in the Rivonia Trial in 1963.

In prison he used his letter-writing and study privileges to the maximum extent. Always he read with a pen in hand, taking notes, annotating. He used his letters to engage with domestic space as best he could, addressing every detail of the lives of children, grandchildren, relatives and, of course, his wife. He would draft each letter in a notebook, edit it and then transcribe it onto sheets of paper. The notebooks remained his record of all his epistolary writing. He kept other notebooks, and later simple diaries. And he directed a deluge of paper at the prison authorities. A number of the political prisoners' struggles were accompanied by written demands, petitions and letters of authorization to lawyers. Many of these instruments were either written by or channelled through Mandela. Today the archives of the South

African state contain a dense record of Mandela's years in prison and attest to the extent to which use of the records provided critical leverage in extracting concessions.

Some of the concessions were big; others very small. All of them demonstrated the power of the record. In 1970, for example, Mandela asked for a supply of honey to help with his treatment for high blood pressure. What followed was a long back-and-forth, with Mandela demonstrating politeness, a refusal ever to accept 'no' for an answer and a willingness to slip into Afrikaans in order to optimize leverage. Despite expressions of official consternation in the prison file, including expletives, Mandela got his honey.

Keeping records was to become a daily discipline of extreme importance to him after his release from prison. He was almost seventy-two years old, no longer used to constant travel, a diary crammed with meetings, and political processes of extreme complexity and instability. He had assistants, of course, but he insisted on keeping his own notes. The archive is full of his notebooks from the period 1990 to 1994, some of them customized for him, others picked up from stationery stores or hotel rooms. They became a vital tool in enabling him to stay on top of an ever-shifting reality. He was still completely in charge.

And he was someone who always had a pen to hand. He almost had a fetish about pens. A certain obsessiveness. He would insist on using his fountain pen for writing tasks of particular significance to him. For instance, when he sat down in 1998 to start a new memoir, a reflection on his presidency, he wrote the whole of the first chapter with it. Later drafts of the chapter – and there were many – were all written with a ballpoint. In 2005, he sat with then Minister of Arts and Culture Pallo Jordan on a platform outside the museum in Mthatha, to donate his presidential gifts and awards to the state in front of a large audience. The organizers had prepared two silver ballpoint pens for the occasion, each one inscribed accordingly. Jordan took his and started signing the deeds of donation. Mandela scrutinized his ballpoint and shook his head, saying that he would prefer to sign such an important document with his fountain pen. For him this was not simply a question of taste. It was more about simple principles and simple disciplines. Ones which could be translated into an essential power.

When he started formalizing his personal archive with the Nelson Mandela Foundation in 2004, it was questions of power which preoccupied him. He didn't want it to become another means by which he was elevated in the public imagination. He didn't want it to be a vanity project. Instead, he committed it to continuing processes of restoration and reconciliation in South Africa. And,

> *most importantly, we want it to dedicate itself to the recovery of memories and stories suppressed by power. That is the call of justice. The call which must be the project's most important shaping influence.*[15]

Time, Body and Soul

Mandela accessed another source of essential energy, and arguably power, through a range of daily disciplines. He took care of himself. He cared about the way he looked and the way he was seen. Even in the midst of the greatest clamour as a global icon and leader of demanding processes, he had his routines and he always kept an eye on his watch. There was a deliberateness about everything he did. He detested disrespect for punctuality. Time was a precious resource to be tended, both for self and for others. He could be obsessive about it.

Mandela always liked to be early. Not for him the indulgence of very important persons who expect the less exalted to wait for them. He reserved a special anger, sometimes a fury, for those who kept him and others waiting. On one occasion a well-known leader felt his wrath when the leader arrived very late for an event at which he was a speaker. When Mandela stood up to speak after him, he began with an extended homily on the importance of punctuality.

Perhaps the one day on which he could have been expected to be a little tardy, a little less disciplined, was the morning after his release from prison. The previous day had been a full and punishing one. He walked out of Victor Verster Prison after waiting many hours for the arrival of his wife Winnie.[xxiii]

'Good wise leaders respect the law and basic values of their society.'

– Nelson Mandela

He was frustrated by the delay. And then followed the many dramas of his first speech from the Cape Town City Hall and the evening at the home of Archbishop and Leah Tutu. He retired to bed much later than usual. Trevor Manuel, who was a member of the team which 'received' Mandela from prison and had not slept for the better part of two days, recalls returning home and collapsing into bed, only to be woken at 4 a.m. by the phone ringing. It was Mandela, up at his usual time and wondering where his exercise weights were.[16]

Staying physically fit was a priority throughout his life. He was careful about what he ate and drank. He hardly ever indulged. As a youth, he played a range of sports and trained hard for them. In adulthood, he favoured the boxing gym with its particular ethos and routines. While in prison, he often irritated his comrades by waking them early as he rose to run on the spot in his cell. He took pride in being lean and strong. When he was stripped naked by warders together with a large group of other detainees in the lead-up to the Treason Trial in 1956, he chuckled to

himself at the appearance of many of them.[xxiv]
Late in life he would often tease old friends,
comrades and associates whose stomachs
were sagging visibly. 'It's not healthy,' he'd say,
patting his own still-hard midriff.

Looking good, having style, dressing
well. He understood that one's dress, one's
appearance, was a basic tool of one's trade.
As a prefect in high school his uniform was
immaculate and his hair cut with the then-
fashionable large shaved side parting. As a
young lawyer and rising anti-apartheid activist,
he was always dressed in impeccable suits
and had a cigarette lazily to hand. As an old
man, by then almost always wearing what had
become the world-famous 'Madiba shirt' –
which gave him a powerful and almost
unique brand – he would often complain to
his assistants about their smoking habits.
Eventually one of them produced a large
photograph from the 1950s featuring him
with cigarette in hand. 'No,' he said with a
trademark glint of mischief in his eye, 'to
be a big man in those days you had to be a
smoker. But I wasn't really smoking.'

Image mattered. Arguably he understood branding better than anyone else and earlier than most. After his capture in 1962 by the apartheid state, he adopted a strategy of non-cooperation for his trial. He wore traditional Thembu dress in the courtroom, refused the services of a defence lawyer, and rejected the legitimacy of the process because he was 'a black man in a white man's court'. The symbolism was powerful, the message compelling. In his years underground, he had fostered the image of an elusive revolutionary, and came to be called 'the Black Pimpernel'. Part of the image was a revolutionary full but raggedy beard. Shortly before his arrest, he was advised by comrades to shave it off, precisely because it had become so distinctive. But he had become attached to it and was wearing it when he was captured. Dress was a tool of his trade. But it was also the garment of his soul.

Befriending Mortality

Most famously, Nelson Mandela and the other Rivonia trialists[xxv] faced down death in

1964. They fully expected the death penalty and as a political strategy chose not to seek mitigation. But this was the endpoint of a long process for all of them. As activists taking on the increasingly brutal apartheid regime, they had all chosen a path of extreme danger. Taking up armed struggle against the regime three years earlier had put them directly in the firing line. And for the black comrades, there was the reality of a lifetime negotiating systems in which black lives did not matter. Mortality, for them, was woven into the warp and weft of daily life.

In his twilight years, despite strong taboos against doing so, he spoke often to those around him about dying. We remember a day towards the end of his life, a December day, when he called all the Nelson Mandela Foundation staff into his office in order to thank them for their service during the year. It was his normal practice as the year came to an end. 'This might be the last time,' he said, 'because I am ancient now. You know, when I get to the pearly gates, they will ask me, "Who are you?" I will say, "Madiba!" They will respond, "Where do you come from?" I will say, "South Africa!" "Ah," they will say, "you are *that* Madiba. No, you have come to the wrong gates. You see those ones far away down there, the very warm ones? Those are your gates."' A pause, before he concluded, 'But don't worry. Big business and the ANC will be there to assist me.' And then, of course, the vintage Nelson Mandela laugh.

Talking about his own mortality, at one level, was certainly about him enabling those close to him to make peace with the fact that he would not always be around. He was helping them. Using, if you like, a discipline of generosity. But at another level he was also demonstrating a lifetime of befriending the death that is always part of life. And into his nineties he had honed this ancient human discipline. One of the hardest of all.

'Leadership falls into two categories. Those who are inconsistent, whose actions cannot be predicted, who agree today on a major [issue] and repudiate it the following day. Those who are consistent, who have a sense of honour, a vision.'

– Nelson Mandela

Ordinary Stuff

Discipline and principle gave Nelson Mandela the space within which he crafted his genius. This extraordinary leader was fashioned out of the ordinary stuff life offers to human beings. Anyone can learn the disciplines of listening, of recording, of staying fit and so on. Anyone can embrace the principles of respecting otherness and befriending mortality. Anyone can find the leader within themselves. Mandela's instincts as a politician, his exquisite timing, his capacity to take the opportunities presented by contingency and happenstance, grew very precisely out of his painstaking, daily engagement with this ordinary stuff, often in the most debilitating of circumstances. He was always in for the long haul. Twenty-seven years in prison. Forty-six years of study to get his LLB degree. Forty-eight years in the ANC to rise to become its president. He knew how to endure.

In boxing parlance, Mandela possessed the magic of balance. Like every great boxer – a Muhammad Ali, a Sugar Ray Robinson, a Baby Jake Matlala – he floated like a butterfly and stung like a bee. The key was balance. He could dance away from danger and slip punches. He could equally well lean on the ropes, absorbing punishment. And he knew how to jab accurately or deliver the knock-out blow. But what people saw in the ring grew out of what they didn't see – the hard yards he put in on the road and in the gym. The daily disciplines, the slog, the empty training rings, the fraying punch-balls and neglected loved ones. To float like a butterfly and sting like a bee, one has always already had to have worked like an ant.

For Mandela, surprisingly perhaps, 'consistency' was the underlying quality of good leadership. As he once insisted: 'Leadership falls into two categories. Those who are inconsistent, whose actions cannot be predicted, who agree today on a major [issue] and repudiate it the following day, [and those] who are consistent, who have a sense of honour, a vision.'[17] Staying with the metaphor of boxing best enables us to appreciate his point. In the triad of floating like a butterfly, stinging like a bee, working like an ant, it is the latter which provides the underlying durability of every great boxer as well as the capacity to perform consistently at the highest level. (Ironically, it also enhances an ability to do the unpredictable when necessary – a critical weapon in the arsenal of both boxer and politician.)

For the work of an ant – the daily disciplines of conduct, routine and practice – Mandela drew deeply on multiple traditions, institutions and mentors. As we have argued, from early in life he demonstrated a capacity to test every rule he encountered and either adopt it as his own or discard it. In doing so, he fashioned for himself a unique fusion of influences and created what we are calling that 'fecund space' in which good timing and instinct flourish. Precisely the space – to return to where we started – which enabled him from prison in 1986 to see the opportunity for a game-changing intervention and then to take charge of it against all the odds. He knew how to lead.

'A real leader uses every issue, no matter how serious and sensitive, to ensure that at the end of the debate we should emerge stronger and more united than ever before.'

– Nelson Mandela

About Nelson Mandela

Nelson Mandela was born in the Transkei, South Africa, on 18 July 1918. He joined the African National Congress in the early 1940s and was engaged in struggles against the ruling National Party's apartheid system for many years before being arrested in August 1962. Mandela was incarcerated for more than twenty-seven years, during which his reputation as a potent symbol of resistance for the anti-apartheid movement grew steadily. Released from prison in 1990, Mandela was jointly awarded the Nobel Peace Prize in 1993, and became South Africa's first democratically elected president in 1994. He died on 5 December 2013, at the age of ninety-five.

NELSON MANDELA
FOUNDATION
Living the legacy

About the Nelson Mandela Foundation

The Nelson Mandela Foundation is a non-profit organization founded by Nelson Mandela in 1999 as his post-presidential office. In 2007 he gave it a mandate to promote social justice through dialogue and memory work.

Its mission is to contribute to the making of a just society by mobilizing the legacy of Nelson Mandela, providing public access to information on his life and times and convening dialogue on critical social issues.

The Foundation strives to weave leadership development into all aspects of its work.

nelsonmandela.org

About the Project

'A true leader must work hard to ease tensions, especially when dealing with sensitive and complicated issues. Extremists normally thrive when there is tension, and pure emotion tends to supersede rational thinking.'

– Nelson Mandela

Inspired by Nelson Mandela, *I Know This to Be True* was conceived to record and share what really matters for the most inspiring leaders of our time.

I Know This to Be True is a Nelson Mandela Foundation project anchored by original interviews with twelve different and extraordinary leaders each year, for five years – six men and six women – who are helping and inspiring others through their ideas, values and work.

Royalties from sales of this book will support language translation and free access to films, books and educational programmes using material from the series, in all countries with developing economies, or economies in transition, as defined by United Nations annual classifications.

iknowthistobetrue.org

The People Behind the Project

'A good head and a good heart are always a formidable combination.'

– Nelson Mandela

For the Nelson Mandela Foundation:
Sello Hatang, Verne Harris, Noreen Wahome, Razia Saleh and Sahm Venter

For Blackwell & Ruth:
Geoff Blackwell, Ruth Hobday, Cameron Gibb, Nikki Addison, Olivia van Velthooven, Elizabeth Blackwell, Kate Raven, Annie Cai and Tony Coombe

We hope that together we can help to mobilize Madiba's extraordinary legacy, to the benefit of communities around the world.

Acknowledgements

For over a decade now we have been giving guided tours of the Nelson Mandela Foundation, including sessions in the archive, and we are grateful to the people from many parts of the world who have posed probing questions about the qualities that made Madiba the leader he became. Perhaps the most difficult questions have been offered by members of student formations and local communities in South Africa. They became the initial stimulus to developing a text that could be used without tour guides.

Of course, our greatest debt is to Madiba himself, who made his archive available and gave the two of us his own time so generously. It was good to work for him, but best of all was simply to listen to him. It is our hope that we listened well.

Colleagues at the Foundation have provided us with unstinting support. Special thanks to Razia Saleh and her archives team, senior researcher Sahm Venter, chief operating officer Limpho Monyamane and chief executive personal assistant Buyi Sishuba.

The idea for a little book like this was germinated in conversations with Geoff Blackwell and Ruth Hobday, publishers with the rare quality of thinking about soul rather than profit. We trust we haven't disappointed you. We are also grateful to your colleagues Cameron Gibb, Nikki Addison, Olivia van Velthooven, Elizabeth Blackwell and Mike Wagg, who honoured your commitment to excellence.

Mandla Langa provided insight and affirmation in the early stages of writing, soon after he had undertaken the major task of authoring what became the book on Madiba's presidency *Dare Not Linger: The Presidential Years.* It was an honour to work with you.

For the fundamental insight that all human beings are called to leadership, whatever their station and wherever they are positioned, we are grateful to the Tutu Leadership Fellowship, the Global Leadership Academy project (GLAC) at the Deutsche Gesellschaft für Internationale Zusammenarbeit (GIZ) GmbH (German Society for International Cooperation), Obenewa Amponsah, Achmat Dangor, Rebecca Freese, Chandre Gould, Zelda la Grange, Jerry Mabena, Graça Machel, Jabu Mashinini, Njabulo Ndebele, Pat Pillai, Leon Wessels, Peter Westoby and Undine Whande.

To finding the leader within, especially when one is feeling completely lost.

Sello Hatang and Verne Harris

Notes

i   Madiba is Mandela's clan name.

ii Pollsmoor Maximum Security Prison, Cape Town. Mandela was imprisoned there along with Walter Sisulu, Raymond Mhlaba, Andrew Mlangeni and, later, Ahmed Kathrada from March 1982 to August 1988.

iii Mandela began meeting with then Minister of Justice Kobie Coetsee in 1985 to request a meeting to begin discussing the possibility of talks between the government and the ANC.

iv Chief Jongintaba Dalindyebo (d. 1942), the regent of the Thembu people. He became Mandela's guardian following his father's death.

v   Mandela was born in the Thembu kingdom and was a member of the royal household.

vi The ANC didn't open its membership to non-Africans until 1967, but had worked with other groups in what became known as the Congress movement comprising the ANC, South African Indian Congress, South African Coloured People's Congress and Congress of Democrats.

vii Prison guard, or warden.

viii Mandela kept detailed diaries throughout his life. During his presidential years, he would often write notes in the desk diary which kept the details of his schedule to record minutes of meetings.

ix Mandela, along with nine others, was put on trial between 1963 and 1964 for sabotage in the Rivonia Trial, named after the suburb of Rivonia, Johannesburg, South Africa, where six of the nine were arrested. Mandela and seven of his fellow trialists were imprisoned in Robben Island Prison.

x   Thembisile (Chris) Hani (1942–93), was an anti-apartheid activist and freedom fighter who was assassinated outside his home in Johannesburg, South Africa, in 1993.

xi Makgatho (Kgatho) Mandela (1950–2005), Mandela's second-born son to his first wife, Evelyn, who died of AIDS complications on 6 January 2005 in Johannesburg, South Africa.

xii See Prologue, p. 15, paragraph 1.

xiii   Robben Island Maximum Security Prison was situated on an island in Table Bay, seven kilometres off the coast of Cape Town. Mandela was first sent there in May 1963 and again on 13 June 1964 after being convicted of sabotage in the Rivonia Trial. He was imprisoned there until 1982, when he was transferred to Pollsmoor Maximum Security Prison on the mainland.

xiv   Oliver Reginald (O. R.) Tambo (1917–93), lawyer, politician, anti-apartheid activist, and freedom fighter. Co-founder, with Mandela, of one of South Africa's first African legal practices.

xv   Mvuyelwa Thabo Mbeki (1942–), politician and anti-apartheid activist. Deputy president of South Africa 1994–99, president of South Africa 1999–2008.

xvi   In what became known as the Shell House Massacre, eight members of the IFP were shot dead during a march outside Shell House, the ANC's headquarters in Johannesburg, South Africa,, on 28 March 1994. They were protesting against the upcoming elections that the IFP was proposing to boycott. In an eleventh-hour deal the organization agreed to participate in the first democratic elections on 27 April 1994.

xvii   Ruth First (1925–82), journalist and Communist Party and ANC activist, fellow accused in the 1956 Treason Trial. She went into exile in 1964 and was killed by a parcel bomb sent by apartheid agents while she was living in Mozambique.

xviii   Bantu Stephen Biko (1946–77), co-founder and first president of the South African Students' Organization (SASO) formed in 1968–9, which later became the Black People's Convention (BPC). The Black Consciousness Movement (BCM) was born out the political vacuum left by the banning of the ANC and the Pan Africanist Congress (PAC) in 1960, and the detention and imprisonment of political leaders during the 1960s. Starting with the formation of SASO, it spread into wider society with the BPC and the South African Students' Movement (SASM) in 1972, and was central to the 1976 Student Uprising which began in Soweto. Biko is widely viewed as the leader of the BCM. He was murdered on 12 September 1977 whilst in police custody.

xix   Ahmed Kathrada (1929–2017), leading member of the ANC and South African Communist Party, and fellow Rivonia trialist who was imprisoned with Mandela.

xx   Sathyandranath (Mac) Maharaj (1935–), freedom fighter, academic,
        politician, anti-apartheid activist, and fellow Robben Island prisoner
        and former comrade.

xxi   'Dagga' is a South African term for cannabis.

xxii   Tim Couzens (1944–2016), historian and author. He interviewed
        Mandela a number of times during this period as part of the research
        team for Mandela's book *Conversations with Myself*.

xxiii   Victor Verster Prison, a low-security prison located between Paarl and
        Franschhoek in the Western Cape. Mandela was transferred there
        in 1988, and lived in a house inside the prison compound until his
        release in 1990.

xxiv   The Treason Trial (1956–61) was a result of the apartheid government's
        attempt to quell the power of the Congress Alliance, a coalition of
        anti-apartheid organisations. In early-morning raids on 5 December
        1956, 156 individuals were arrested and charged with high treason.
        By the end of the trial in March 1961 all the accused either had the
        charges withdrawn or, in the case of the last twenty-eight accused
        (including Mandela), were acquitted.

xxv   A South African term for a defendant in a court trial.

Sources and Permissions

For more information about Nelson Mandela, visit the Nelson Mandela Foundation's website at https://www.nelsonmandela.org.

A comprehensive list of books by or about Nelson Mandela can be found at https://www.nelsonmandela.org/publications.

Image galleries, videos and other media about Nelson Mandela can be found at https://www.nelsonmandela.org/multimedia/.

Mandela's speeches cited below, together with many others, can be viewed at https://www.nelsonmandela.org/content/page/speeches.

1   Verne Harris, in conversation with George Bizos, Johannesburg, South Africa, circa 2010.
2   Nelson Mandela, *Long Walk to Freedom* (London, England: Abacus, 1995), pp. 25–6.
3   NM, speech to the court, Old Synagogue, Pretoria, South Africa, 22 October 1962, see http://db.nelsonmandela.org/speeches/pub_view.asp?pg=item&ItemID=NMS011.
    NM, speech from the dock at the opening of the defence case, Rivonia Trial, Pretoria Supreme Court, Pretoria, South Africa, 20 April 1964, see http://db.nelsonmandela.org/speeches/pub_view.asp?pg=item&ItemID=NMS010.
    NM, speech after his release, City Hall, Cape Town, South Africa, 11 February 1990, see http://db.nelsonmandela.org/speeches/pub_view.asp?pg=item&ItemID=NMS016.
    NM, televised address to the nation after the assassination of Chris Hani, Johannesburg, South Africa, 13 April 1993, see http://db.nelsonmandela.org/speeches/pub_view.asp?pg=item&ItemID=NMS135.
    NM, speech at his inauguration as President of South Africa, Union Buildings, Pretoria, South Africa, 10 May 1994, see http://db.nelsonmandela.org/speeches/pub_view.asp?pg=item&ItemID=NMS176.
4   NM, closing address at the XIII International AIDS Conference, Durban, South Africa, 14 July 2000, http://db.nelsonmandela.org/speeches/pub_view.asp?pg=item&ItemID=NMS083.
5   *Mandela: The Authorised Portrait* (Auckland, New Zealand: PQ Blackwell, 2006), p. 334.
6   NM, *Long Walk to Freedom* (London, England: Abacus, 1995), p. 749.
7   NM, from a letter to Winnie Mandela, dated 9 December 1979, see *Conversations with Myself* (London, England: Macmillan, 2010), p. 234.

8   *Mandela at 90*, directed by Clifford Bestall (UK: Giant Media Productions, 2008).

9   NM in conversation with Richard Stengel, Johannesburg, South Africa, 16 March 1993, CD 28, Nelson Mandela Foundation, Johannesburg, South Africa.

10   NM, *Long Walk to Freedom* (London, England: Abacus, 1995), p. 36.

11   NM, interview with Tim Couzens, Verne Harris and Mac Maharaj for *Mandela: The Authorised Portrait*, 2006, Johannesburg, South Africa, 13 August 2005.

12   Ibid.

13   NM, *Conversations with Myself* (Macmillan, London, England, 2010), p. 409.

14   Bruno Latour, "Visualization and Cognition: Thinking with Eyes and Hands", *Knowledge and Society* 6:1–40, 1986.

15   NM, speech at the launch of the Nelson Mandela Centre of Memory and Commemoration Project, Nelson Mandela Foundation, Johannesburg, South Africa, 21 September 2004, http://db.nelsonmandela.org/speeches/pub_view.asp?pg=item&ItemID=NMS761.

16   See *Choice, Not Fate: The Life and Times of Trevor Manuel*, Pippa Green (Johannesburg, South Africa: Penguin Books (South Africa) (Pty) Ltd, 2008), p. 315.

17   NM, from a notebook, date unknown.

The publisher is grateful for literary permissions to reproduce items subject to copyright which have been used with permission. Every effort has been made to trace the copyright holders and the publisher apologizes for any unintentional omission. We would be pleased to hear from any not acknowledged here and undertake to make all reasonable efforts to include the appropriate acknowledgement in any subsequent edition.

Pages 6, 13, 17, 27, 36, 45, 52, 61, 67, 74, 81, 83: *Nelson Mandela by Himself: The Authorised Book of Quotations* edited by Sello Hatang and Sahm Venter (Pan Macmillan: Johannesburg, South Africa, 2017), copyright © 2011 Nelson R. Mandela and the Nelson Mandela Foundation, used by permission of the Nelson Mandela Foundation, Johannesburg, South Africa; pp. 26, 33, 46: *Long Walk to Freedom* by Nelson Mandela (Abacus: London, England, 1995), copyright © Nelson R. Mandela, used by permission of the Nelson Mandela Foundation, Johannesburg, South Africa; p. 32: Nelson Mandela closing address at the XIII International AIDS Conference, Durban, South Africa, 14 July 2000, copyright © Nelson Mandela Foundation, used by permission of the Nelson Mandela Foundation, Johannesburg, South Africa; pp. 34, 50: *Conversations with Myself* by Nelson Mandela (Macmillan: London, England, 2010), copyright © 2010 Nelson R. Mandela and the Nelson Mandela Foundation, used by permission of the Nelson Mandela Foundation, Johannesburg, South Africa; p. 39: recordings of *Mandela at 90*, directed by Clifford Bestall (UK: Giant Media Productions, 2008), copyright © Nelson R. Mandela, used by permission of the Nelson Mandela Foundation; p. 40: recordings of Nelson Mandela in conversation with Richard Stengel (Johannesburg, South Africa: Nelson Mandela Foundation, 1992–3), copyright © Nelson R. Mandela, used by permission of the Nelson Mandela Foundation; p. 54: "Visualization and Cognition: Thinking with Eyes and Hands", Bruno Latour, *Knowledge and Society* 6:1–40, 1986, used with permission; p. 58: Nelson Mandela speech at the launch of the Nelson Mandela Centre of Memory and Commemoration Project, Nelson Mandela Foundation, Johannesburg, South Africa, 21 September 2004, copyright © Nelson Mandela Foundation, used by permission of the Nelson Mandela Foundation, Johannesburg, South Africa; p. 72: a notebook by Nelson Mandela, date unknown, copyright © Nelson R. Mandela, used by permission of the Nelson Mandela Foundation, Johannesburg, South Africa.

About the Authors

Sello Hatang

Sello Hatang is chief executive of the Nelson Mandela Foundation. Previously he was the head of information communications and spokesperson for the South African Human Rights Commission. He participated in the post-apartheid transformation of the National Archives of South Africa, including providing archival support for the Truth and Reconciliation Commission which was established in 1995 to investigate apartheid-era crimes. He is a former director of the South African History Archive (SAHA) at the University of the Witwatersrand in Johannesburg, and has served on the boards of the Advisory Council of the Council for the Advancement of the South African Constitution (CASAC), SAHA, and the Open Democracy Advice Centre. He co-edited *Nelson Mandela by Himself: The Authorised Book of Quotations*.

Hatang was awarded an honorary diploma by the city of Buenos Aires, Argentina, in 2017 in recognition of his leadership. In 2019 he was given the Keys to the City of Florence, Italy, for his work in human rights and promoting the legacy of Nelson Mandela, and received the Journalists and Writers Foundation Culture of Peace Award.

Verne Harris

Verne Harris heads the Nelson Mandela Foundation's leadership and knowledge development processes, and was Mandela's archivist from 2004 to 2013. A former deputy director of the National Archives of South Africa, he served in the Truth and Reconciliation Commission and is an adjunct professor at the Nelson Mandela University in Port Elizabeth and an honorary research fellow with the University of Cape Town, South Africa. He has served as a board member for *Archival Science*, the Ahmed Kathrada Foundation, the Freedom of Expression Institute, and the South African History Archive.

Harris has authored or co-authored five books, of which his two novels were shortlisted for South Africa's M-Net Literary Awards. He is the recipient of archival publication awards from Australia, Canada and South Africa, and led the editorial team for Nelson Mandela's bestselling book, *Conversations with Myself*. He was awarded an honorary doctorate from the National University of Córdoba, Argentina, in 2014, and held the 2018–9 Follet Chair at Dominican University in Illinois, USA.

First published in the United States of America in 2020 by Chronicle Books LLC.

Produced and originated by
Blackwell and Ruth Limited
Suite 405, Ironbank,150 Karangahape Road
Auckland 1010, New Zealand
www.blackwellandruth.com

Publisher: Geoff Blackwell
Editor in Chief & Project Editor: Ruth Hobday
Design Director: Cameron Gibb
Designer & Production Coordinator: Olivia van Velthooven
Publishing Manager: Nikki Addison
Digital Publishing Manager: Elizabeth Blackwell

Images by Andrew Zuckerman, copyright © Nelson R. Mandela
Layout and design copyright © 2020 Blackwell and Ruth Limited

Text by Sello Hatang and Verne Harris, copyright © 2020 the Nelson Mandela
Foundation. Acknowledgements for permission to reprint previously published
and unpublished material can be found on page 93.

Library of Congress Cataloging-in-Publication Data available.

ISBN 978-1-7972-0017-0

Chronicle Books LLC
680 Second Street
San Francisco, CA 94107
www.chroniclebooks.com

10 9 8 7 6 5 4 3 2 1

Manufactured in China by 1010 Printing Ltd.

Also available in the series: